Eggs

BY FANNY HOWE

FORTY WHACKS
EGGS

EGGS

Poems by Fanny Howe

Houghton Mifflin Company Boston 1970

Library of Congress Catalog Card Number: 70–120837
Printed in the United States of America

Some of the poems in this volume have been published
previously, as follows: *Antioch Review:* "The Sunny Moon
Song." *The Atlantic Monthly:* "Europa's Letter" and
"Afterword." Doubleday Anchor Books: "Jasmine and the
Gypsies," "Two Shots: A Love Affair," and "The Corn
Dance" reprinted from the anthology *Quickly Aging Here,*
edited by Geof Hewitt. *The Harvard Advocate:* "Let's
Pretend," copyright © 1970 by The Harvard Advocate.
The Lyric: "Looking On," under the title "I Watched
My Mother." *Mademoiselle:* "Framed." *The Massachusetts
Review:* "Confessions of Persephone." *Sumac:* "Last Word"
and "Not Dead Yet," the latter under the title "The Living
Theater."

for C. S. & A. M. S.

CONTENTS

I

UNLOVED

I am just seventeen
& it is spring.
I have hung my lilacs
like a wreath
beside the door.

They ask for you
to feel passion for me.
Look how many tricks
I do to make you smile
you with the butter-

scotch skin & drunken
friends. Christmas
hangs in fog
but I can see it
for miles; my parents
call me home

for holly red bulbs
& snow. I go, I go —
& you are there.
You slip & fall
I love you even more.

If only you knew
if only you knew how well
I listen to you.
No one finds more in
your words than I.

Leaves crackle
like insects as I run
to the Russian
Tea Room. You are waiting
with your girl

whose lips slip open
like magazines.
I remember her name
& everywhere you've been . . .
Should you forget

just ask me.

ENLARGEMENTS

1.

Harvey made a painting
green and black
He did it long ago —
but tonight I see
a leafy tree
growing through my wall.

2.

Tonight fear expands me:
people I love are drunk birds
pecking red cherries
and staring the scarecrow
hard in the eye. The scarecrow
tries to fly
but hangs in the tree:
lynched and drawn.

3.

I loom from my shadow
a strip of dark bark
peeled from the side
of a conifer. Green
and hungry the nest
of birds in my hair.

4.

My lead is a seed
and my pencil
is a complex weed

planting as it grows
Who says
I'm not equal to
a tree.

5.
Bells ring from
the streetlight's
direction.
Pain is illumination
and short-lived.

6.
There is always
someone strange
waiting
to meet you
at the end.

ANNA AKHMATOVA

The weight of your poems is
like arms around my neck

There's tense and healing
power in this common knot

You've been as quiet as earth
as faithful as seasons

for ten odd years my friend

There is in your words
a tone so familiar —

serious (like someone alone
with nowhere to go) —

you'd know me as your own.
If only I could call you

mother!

HEAD STONE

Milk spilled
and lit up our tears
too late.

Glass splintered
under foot
in underwear and shoes.

I watched
your overcoat swing shut
on dynamite.

You said
oil would turn into fire
south of each border

whether I liked it
or not.
I did, but you left.

Since then
I haven't stopped acting
the same,

begging for change.

A REASON TO STAY

April is trumping up
        camouflage
    slowly this year
I want to disappear
        but even
with leaves & flowers
painting me I'd be
    longing waiting
        for you
    which is why
I'm this full of fear

AFTERWORD

Thrice I croaked
before the sun was up;
the scared bed jumped
to catch my falls; and
the mouth in the shade
exposed a galaxy of snow.

Surprise: the sky was tinsel
on the Christmas trees.
I made an angel of myself
and hung from an icicle
choking. Since you went off
the sun is black sackcloth.

Everything was religious
then. Even our walk
by factories and riverbeds
produced the kingdom of heaven
with you its hot and tender king,
with me adoring or loving.

Now black winds blow
and take away my breath.
Again the night is dying on my lips.
If only I told you before:
without you I feel
I'm skating past innumerable monuments:

no words,
no facts, no laws to stop my fall.

NORA

I saw her move; she was a quiet girl.
    She stayed awhile
to bind her son into his shoes, and when
her strong Hassidic hands had tied the bow.
    I watched her go
in long gray socks and tweed,
shades of patience in her stride.

    Such darkling curls
and amber skin as hers assembled secrets
that her Spanish tongue increased.
    How little was seen.
She moved with death as with her selfsame son
familiar though unknown. I saw her move;
    then she was gone.

SISTERS

We made a pretty picture
squatting on our knees
where apples were like udders
and cows grew on trees

Buses flew through heaven
and leaves grew on the sea
and raspberries were bleeding
while crowds watched passively.

We called the picture HOME
and brought it to our school
but nobody believed us though
we only told the truth

INDIAN SUMMER

your pleasures
make me love

you: orange
juice   swimming

music   lies &
even women

Oh   & I only
knew the season

when you pulled
up our covers

at dawn   & said
we were freezing.

I KNOW MORE

I know more about your death
than you do.
The doctors gave me
every detail, and after all
I've had plenty of time
to think about it: —
surely more than you!

It's said your death
was done by the time it began.

Like anything else:
stepping over a dull dog,
coughing,
locking a door or
saluting a friend:
you couldn't even say
Jack Robinson.

The authorities add
you couldn't have known it was happening.

But who are they
to say.
My own opinion is
it was one
of your last minute
decisions:
thoughtful, that is.

Remember
I've had plenty of time
to ask how you could
do it:

you might even say
too much.

NOT DEAD YET

Your shadows are warm
your sleeping skin
as soft as ox-hide

Dido built Carthage
on such small land
and burned and burned

So I dread in sleep
your vegetable lips
capturing kisses

from celluloid lovers.
I've opened all my lips
like curtains

at the repertory theater
of my parents
to play out their lives

with you. Don't sleep
We're not dead yet: —
our love is kicking, wet.

THE QUARREL

The ocean is rushing
at the windowpane
and every word
is rising like foam:
direct, indifferent.

I watch from bed
spray spark and sift
in chains down air . . .
Like small renunciations
your footsteps on the stairs.

YELLOW THE SUN

Cardinal colors
give cold rooms heat

& hard chairs comfort.
So on those days

when the going is
rough, count on me

to be how I want
to stay: — a child

with you coloring in
the spaces & lines:

yellow the sun & brown
the house we live in.

THE SUNNY MOON SONG

What are you doing away
the children are sucking
icicles but I have
no one to play with today

If you come with a present
bad news or a friend
that will be okay but don't
come as nothing dead-eyes

All by my lonesome outside
in the snow my cap
and mittens icy come home
is all I can say

What will you bring
I keep wondering waiting
and wondering what you will
bring and if dead-eyes

No nothing is fair
not even a question
but I can't help asking
if you will surprise

me by coming back home
with presents like hands
no never again a surprise
from your ashes and dead-eyes

CHARITY

You paced
the widow's
walk, deep
in the sea
of sleep

You saw
the life
of your love
go down
drowning

Mother
it was then
your child
came in
like charity

and watched
you toss
and sigh
in your wet
white sheets

Her tears
were generous:
as presents
dependent
on suffering.

TIME & PLACE

You had some faith
to lose
& I set out
to prove it wasn't
true; it got
us both
in the end.
This was the way
you looked
for God:
you walked on air
from
Lago di Garda
to
Santa Barbara
— "beds of luxury" —
and thought
He must be there.

Being protestant
your church
was like a roadside
restaurant
(only
the best).
You stopped in
for nourishment.
You had sticky lips
and mats
in your peroxide hair

smoked
a little with your wine: —
virgin.

＊

At the time
you even stood in Paris
eating
apricot tarts
plump
with passion
& respect
before the hems
of Notre Dame.
Poor thing.
No one could escape
your pity.
Indifferent kisses
struck your neck
like hornets,
as milk,
letting down,
stings.

Circumstances
stopped
all that now
you flew American
thru air
touched
Selma Dallas Oakland
later traveled
byways

seen from a train
named
Sparkling Water.
Green mountains
melted
like Jell-O: —
an existential
vision
of the Flood.

*

You left
God necking at dawn
in bed you
said no you said why
being
no feminist
soft for entrance
& landed
on a roof
at dawn
beside a crazy boy
with yellow hair
from there
to shaking snow
off empty arms
in a bar
beside Times Square

Snow fell
like musical notes
on your synthetic
fur.

By now
you salted
your meat
with tears
at any curb or
corner spa.

*

You might as well
be poor.
There must be
a cure
for this
you would say
you would give
your all
to be 3 feet tall
under a sunflower
smelling a cow.
Running
you shared nothing
with children
but lived
in a city
like Christmas

and those
were the days
you were led
by the stars
in your dog's eyes
whose squeals
were fingers

polishing
your mirror.
You were led
again
to Santa Barbara
where
palms & oleander
suffered
from heat, or worms.

     *

Your sky
was falling in
Second to Nothing
the Second Coming
on Nothing
you said
and then
I'm here again
where I've never been
before!
There must be
a cure
for this.
I'm unhappy as
an atheist
and only have God
to blame
for it.

Now salt
& wood
are yours

for superstitions.
Animals
show you
morals.
You smoke
with your gin
yet when grains
of sugar
grow in size
& spill
on your breakfast
cereal
you say
you have the soul
of a child.

*

What choice
what change
came over
you suburbanite
I've come
to say
so long to see
a sky full
of violets fall
on your grave.
Already
decayed
how can you rise
again
like spring?
In fact

I'm amazed
you're still alive
at any time
any place —

war baby.

II

FRESH POND
for my father (1906–1967)

I've come here to hear
what I can
of our conversations
blowing in spirals
of shade. It may be the wind
in the conifers
but I'm trying to hear
what you said, and where.

Now yellow leaves
are moving on the golf green
cemetery. When it was spring
no chicory or aster
grew into my arms and
I never saw the reservoir
so dark:
breakers white as snow
are nipping at the gulls.

Do you realize
we're changing altogether
all together here?
You ought to know your death
has brought the desired
changes.
Will you forgive us
our sudden strength
found in the losing
of memory?

Listen and see:
I'm tracing your steps to hear
what your spare response
would be.

LET'S PRETEND

Suppose you just passed on
to another room
and it was all a joke:
chuckles from the crematorium:
you slip off to Rome.

Some resurrection.
Now it seems you've come in time
for spring
and are surprised that
we don't know how to react

to your tricks.
Well, you missed the end
of a lot of stories;
and I guess you have new memories
you can't repeat.

Suppose we sit on the lawn
talking politics instead.
Some introductions:
this is my husband
and *this was your wife.*

She hasn't been the same
since we stood
in the snow, crying
over you. All appetites gone . . .
Oh don't, please, come back again.

THE LAODICEANS

Our house shakes
on stilts,
our neighbors have drawn
the shades
and turned their music up.
Nearby, like them,
a grave
has its troubles:
flowers fly from the stone
(*Tommy Died Trying*)
over the cliff
to drown. Today's
blue mussels are black.

The terrible troubles
of others
come flying with the hawk;
they shake
the stiff-necked body
of the customs house
the witch's house,
and our tender property.
Love, stay away; my sleep
is no longer sweet.
I hear
the whispers of those

in pain,
in morgues, hospitals,
halfway between,

the sobs
of the homeless landlocked
unloved.
They ride on this wind
from a country
in chaos: human voices
whose anonymous losses,
as potent as gains,
will change our land, and us.

ARRANGEMENTS AT APPOMATTOX

We imagine the two
of them
pacing green lawns:
abstract
black patches bloom
and snowy magnolia
sticks to them.
Azaleas like crinolines
bounce on wind.
People arrange
all the tables and chairs
for the war:
the horns are nearly blowing.
Hornets suck honey
from flaglike flowers.
Together
the two in a tent
meet without plans
having arranged and fulfilled
the event.
Were those the days
when sympathy
came to passion,
without desire,
we would imagine
the brown skin lady sitting
in pink cotton
picked by the two
together smiling.
We would imagine him

young and fair
his buttons pressed against
their aching chests,
the two of them
tasting each other's skin
familiar, sweet.

Instead we imagine the people
outside
pasting confectionary sugar-
white valentines
in memory books.
Sad the horns low
and nickering horses
are saddled,
ready to go: a cannonball
pops like champagne.
The ladies applaud,
the husbands grow stern.
Inside the tent
the man with the gun
gives the orders.
The woman, knees up,
shudders.
Later it comes
to this:
a man who loves her
shoulders
the life of the child
with the golden skin
and calls him brother.

THE HABIT

She has made a habit
of goodness, bringing it

to town & home again
a lady monk a worker

traveling on trolleys
singing DAWN

She has made a habit
of goodness/it fits

her now like skin
We never have to ask

her for a thing: instead
she's heard to whisper

thank you very much
and this is always after

she's helped somebody out.

THE CORN DANCE

1.

She made her appearance at noon.
Soft bells jingled,
like cotton
with drums; silver fox fur
sprigs of evergreen
on limbs soaked red for
the corn dance, August.

Her baby was stripped
of flesh
swaddled in furs and bells, rusted.
She heard through cotton
his small feet
on the soft dust pounding
and all his fathers calling oh.

Once she revived him
with yucca and gourd
or wild aster, his favorite blue.
Once she could feed him
sunflowers.
The sun was their forest;
she couldn't see the trees for the sky.

When the Spanish came
with laces, mosaics and knives
the white men entered
smiling.
With her mummified baby,

a broken dish,
under the Catholic altar
they hid like Jews.

Overhead people
ate caviar
their pale fingers stained black.
Fishbones, seashells stuck
in the vegetation
where she fell; her breasts dripped
to feel the skeletal teeth of her child
nip and swill.

2.
Today
in thin ozone we turn
around and landscapes
attach
your hand to mine.
We walk on the ghost of the sea
in scratch and sun.

We go over
the evergreen mountain
our spirits high . . .
below, adobe walls
as angular as cows
are grazing
around a pockmarked skull.

The ocean just dropped
eleven thousand feet.
We can see the sun

set five times
by walking in circles down.
In the shade of aspens
we stop to smoke.

What a miracle
we are here both in the same year.
You might have stayed
in Spain.
Your camera
sees more than your eye, sensations
invisible; you know
you can't see pain.

The soles of our feet
are salted.
You know a baby's skull
and plankton
made this vegetation
what it is today.
Don't ask me why I feel like sand;
watch the dance.

I am a museum,
a zoological garden,
a room full of tourists,
a tourist full of rooms.
Oh and my heart
thumps
before this dance,
the rite of living bones.

MUSEUM OF NATURAL HISTORY

Put your finger
on the atmosphere:
tap it! tap it —

life moves in death
as Logos in flesh.
Fog like white hair

lies over our path.
We see quick starlings
take to the trees

and breathe their song.
This is a sickroom.
Even our wrists

are chained to air.
Not one act is free
of death, or desire.

We pour out our hearts
and pass the skull,
talking of liberty.

FRAMED

The Incas
painted life
as they saw it:
temples of sun,
hills as brown
as skin,
droughts innate
to every setting.
Each hour was noon
where colors
blended to
fuchsia or ochre.
Wherever nature went
art remained.
So the virtue of
inspired industry
shone in
their almond eyes,
still shines,
their brown bodies
etched on time
and framed.

LIVING WITH IT

Not fair no fun
my sneaky brain
has made me down
and out again
    (I saw germinating
      in hell my friend
      no famous names

I wish I'd gone
with Virgil not alone
My eyes became
as dumb as hands
    (But you held on
      numb as an onion
      unforgiving

I'm scared of night
It brings you back
I watch your spook
struggle to walk
    (Dante made this sight
      Christian gave it
      layers of light

But no religion
clears my vision
of you: el olvidado
whom the world wouldn't know
    (My casualty my friend
      please understand: I dream
      therefore I am.

EGGS

"Leda once saw
  an egg
  hidden under a hyacinth."
                — Sappho

She has to be crazy.
Morning rolls an egg
behind her hyacinth:
a perfect secret
perfect solid.

There she stands
peeking through
an indoor acidic iris
(white frost
for each blue petal)
& says her regrets
get sore in winter.

     *

With her mad head &
her blue flower
saying alas! each time
it feels warm
her silver tears
return her strain
delivering one &
the same round egg.

45

(Could she reorder
nature
there would be
no blood
in any egg)

      *

No-love put the ball
of blood in hers.
Just the gall of
the assaulting swan:
hot snow
her sweat salting
her own meat.

Somewhere an idea.

Too late but if she could
believe something else
she'd bear sunyellow chicks
made of cotton
or an easter egg: —
inside
a village
candy for blood or cardboard.

      *

Convinced this
maddest of women
goes out &
takes her seat
behind the hyacinth

to await that
chaotic crack.

(Will it have wings &
a rope for a neck
be white as
its father?
or will it be smooth &
black as an Egyptian
like herself
human?)

It will be
an idea
from *swan*
rapes woman:
a poem.

THINGS FALL APART

I was running from you past empty homes
high on dunes
        through meadows of ocean & grass
A white dog played in foam
a white cow rang a bell
        and my poem had a dream.

Not even a church
would let me in: — doors closed on
        precious things and I only
wanting to ask you can we
be married again
        — But answer with feeling.

If you would just apologize why
all would be
        forgiven! Oh Lordie, earth
is really round. Our dreams
give birth to poems life confirms.
        Somewhere is a center.

LOOKING ON

I watched my mother stride her way
into a greenhouse where she loves
the atmosphere of damp decay
and plants. It was a merry grave.

Around her, flowers bloomed, though most
were not yet wide. She picked her pots
and, holding them like children, lost
her sense of time; and so she stopped.

My mother, in her tweeds and cape,
examined gold lantana, chive,
and leaves with hidden stems. She gazed
at them with distance in her eyes

like hothouse steam, obscuring thought.
She looked amazed, as if there were
a fact she almost had forgot.
I watched, and grew small with care.

III

THE CONFESSIONS OF PERSEPHONE

1.

I hung around my mother's house
thirteen, thirty, three million springs.
At thirteen
it was easy to have a breeze,
let my lion locks unwind in sun.

I didn't want to go down
when in grass
I discovered how sweet I was
in my own hands.
It was the men who bothered me
savoring my tender skin
like a chicken for Thanksgiving.

Summers I stood in the field
picked weeds red as my lips
my tongue slick as an oyster.
I had a gamey smell
which my lolling playmates
said put me high
on the evolutionary scale.

I kissed their feathered necks
until it hurt.
My mother with seductive steps
drifted by the river
            to the bridge.
Left alone with growing pains
the cramps in my branches

buds
       roots repulsively close:
I actually said
"Hades, come up like a father."

2.
The same old dog
was barking on the steps, the same
unruly servant-judges
creaked around.
Another rotten season
       of mist and gloom.
I began to turn thirty.

starvation
resistance   the qualities of unchosen commitment
bad nerves

This is what's known
as déjà vu
       I remember forgetting before.

There were his footsteps on the stairs
the rattling tray.
Hunger made me sick
along with that stinking rich environment.

Hades has a window
for every day in the year.
Three hundred and sixty-five windows
that give on as many views.
The prints by Sesshu
give similar views: mist rising

black branches
snow and blackbirds in rows.

3.
His calves
had a muscular bend I remembered.
I began
to comb the weather from my hair:
old raindrops, pollen, heat
and appleblossoms
scattering patterns on the floor.

When he put his hand
on my heart
I snatched the pomegranate
off the plate
cut my teeth through tough skin
spilled juice on my chin and breasts
consuming six of several seeds
    that cracked in my mouth
            like nuts

I knew what I was doing:
a self-fertility rite.
I showed him my sprigs.
My roots were serious.
They climbed in darkness
through my body vertical.

The half-light hurt
our love coming up
like rain.
It seemed like the gloaming:

the pain in the forest
when the sun turns green.

And mulse was his skin,
honey to my tongue;
his spit was sweet.
I covered his knees
with my wings of hair
when he found the flower
we missed:
a yellow pansy
which panicked us to tears.

I'm really promiscuous.
He's a new man
every time.

4.
When the bottom of the sea
is falling in
        we hang in space
our fingers clinging to the minutes
        of our last meeting.
Hades takes my hand
and draws me up, an earthquake.

My mother is expecting me.

Birth
is pushing me out
        a night of geographical dreams
my cells are turning off
all over the city, blacking out

cement and shadows.
I don't even care if he touched
my heart.

My mother is expecting me.

LAST WORD

Something called Africa
calls to you and I
know nothing
about Africa (just
wild-hearted animals

Now you say there is
something called Africa
not somebody (I can't be
jealous   It has voices
numbers shapes

But we can't go no
money too many walls
too sad   You go instead
and leave me encrusted
a boat in a winter

community of water
Sail far sail free sail
for Homeric cups of gold
Remember I'm no passing
Harpy but Penelope.

CRAZY VOICE

The seaplane cries
like babies
growing wild:
    and rising
    it shadows
those highways
we tired
together

I'd ride
in that plane
to bring you back home:
    and I'd hum
    like a cello
looking for you

But you know I'm strange
and don't dare run
in case we miss
    each other
    again

FATE'S MAN

Wild berries grow
in my hands when I'm nice
but my fingers turn
into shears when I'm not.

I am an ordinary girl
from an ordinary part
of the world. I wear pink skin
like bullet-proof glass.

What happened to my hot-
blooded paws creased
with time and swinging?
What happened to my language?

I am Hitler's mother
and that's enough.
Two-sided eternity erases
my death. I have lived for good

and will: part child,
part ape, part whore.
Give me a name; I've never heard
my voice or seen my face.

THE GARDENER'S WIDOW

Needle my hair.
The threads are twisting
to ground.
Make it pretty
when it stretches
through patches of grass.

Please thread it
in fast
and leave me
knitted, united, stitched
to the garden
he worked with his brown hands.

I know he was cared for
by dogs, bottles,
and drugs —
those doctors to the poor.
It didn't disturb
the order of your good luck.

Oh sew me in.
Red leaves and marigolds
will cover my sleeves.
I'm begging
for death
with consciousness here.

POEM OF JEALOUSY

"These bitches have lips
like cuts
and eyes as moist
as liniments
They smell the salt
of evil
shake it loose and
call it beautiful
They say they're rich
but tortured
and want more
besides my man:
my sympathy
Welcome, patriots
of the human body
the stench
of your adolescence
has set my house
on fire."

LETTER FROM EUROPA

Shy animal
ancient white Leviathan bull,
heavy sinews holding still:
I think I knew that you were Zeus
and stroked your coat whispering
"Bull, come off it,
I see through your disguise," just as
Beauty sighed to Beast
V*a, le magnifique, va ou je vais.*

The scent of undomesticated skin
is innocent. I caught a whiff on you
when we ran into
the spring wind. Horns honked where geese
did once; your grace saved us.
My sweet, you didn't strip to Zeus
until we crossed a sea embracing salt
and rocking.

But now I can't exactly say
what happened yesterday.
We lay, not inert, but nearly so;
your salty fur, now flesh,
lay heavy on my own.
We weren't alone
but never quite together either.
I was really scared.

The matter in your head pressed
next to mine: a different matter

than my own pressed next to yours.
I wanton and you wanting what?
Men to women are mysteries
and as for gods to mortals . . .
well, I loved the flesh,
your shaded smile.

Now I would rather Hera turn me
to a heifer than see you say
goodbye again like that:
shy, lying, sorry, glad.
My response, produced in a flash,
rivers of giggling jargon,
inconsequential to an immortal.

And today I woke up thinking
it's time to get married
or pregnant at least. Out here
alone on the island of Crete.

TWO SHOTS: A LOVE AFFAIR

Before

Will you, love
come to bear
us together

unhappy children?
It will later
be like this:

I'll know how
I found you
till somebody asks.

After

Drinking
a long glass
of pain as purple

as grapes that stained
our lips
last summer

Drinking
ambrosial poison
I'll go on my way

disguised
as a child:
our own unborn.

JASMINE AND THE GYPSIES

1.

Jasmine sees intentions everywhere
She skates up the avenue
wearing shades she sees people through —
right inside
She reads a mind like ice

Circumstances
she says is what brought her here:
not like her will   On the bus
she formulates a truth bouncing
and forgets

Her brightest trait
is playing dumb   Unzipping a smile
with questions
men turn into wizards   For presents
they turn up Tarot cards

All her doctors are *out to lunch*
when she comes in
Twelve pairs of spectacles   pills   new teeth
is what she gets
She shaves herself between the legs.

2.

It's not death honey
scaring me
but hospitals   prisons   traps!   conscious
of being not
alone in that particular emotion

One night I was landed
let's say busted
in jail   called to the king
of the gypsies
him being like my man

So what do you get?
Been stoned
by rain: a drop a sore   Not mercyful!
So long thinking
the king ditched me   Dead

leaves blew in the park
She scuffs
chin up   hands pocketed she drops
on a bench
waiting to get lucky

3.
Today like every day waiting
she holds back
the shade   The radiator steams
like a train
She writes poetry

love poems to nobody   Snow
on beer-colored streetlights
puts her
in the Ice Capades   whirring solo
ballet on black ice for black eyes: nobility

And shining
in the shower her poem changes
colors like her skin
She calls herself a walking globe from Africa
to Ireland

But liveliest her nights when
she hangs
by the window of her dreams gawking
at forms as human
as words.

4.
Black Beauty
otherwise called the king
of the gypsies
got hurt from defending
a girl

others called the slaveholder's wife
White
He said justice is no
accident just
because injustice is

Walking over
to Jasmine's the flowers he brings
are rose red bloodstains
Hey Miss Nightingale! He didn't know
she was in jail

She didn't know
he took her tub   water black hot
Watched his skin: wrinkled fingers
groin   toes: shrink
A body embalmed.

5.
Buttered toast his hands
not the kisses
but that exact
fatherly fragrance
off his skin

It hits her
in trains   bus stations
the gravity of lust
(home!
Oh freedom

that's the chance
to feel
a new kind of pain
But she's stuck
like sleeping eyes

out of such paradise
It's the daily
toast & butter
nostalgia
keeps her down

6.

So. where
did this dollar come
from where will it go
It's like the leaves
that grow & blow

across your haunt Stiff City
No credit no bank
More faith than
you have in yourself
you have

in a floating bill
a number
from nowhere
(maybe pressed
by the President!

For seconds you ponder
which is for sale
that black dress
or this green bill: *like me*
you can pick one up anywhere

7.
It's too late to tell
you which
one I am: two girls are smoking
stretch our legs
inside our linen tent

Closed for the day: —
you'd say only babies
sleep in the sun
or their mothers' arms
We live for the moment

that passed
It's too late to tell you
my name: —
not Goody Two Shoes
in moccasins

Pocahontas or anyone's
spy
just one of
the girls: —
normal in the extreme.